STEP 1:

If you're stupid, you'll need to know that the most important thing about going abroad is choosing where to go.

Where shall I go?

ICELAND ✕
GREENLAND ✕
SWITZERLAND ✕
INDIA ✕ (Too Far!)
TURKEY ✕ (Too Xmassy!)
PIZZALAND ✕
(FRANCE) ✓ ✓ ✓

(Which is 500 degrees in English temperature!)

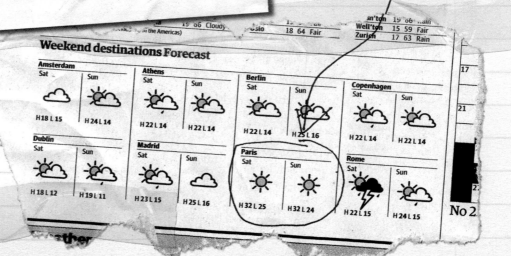

Weekend destinations Forecast

Amsterdam	**Athens**	**Berlin**	**Copenhagen**
Sat / Sun	Sat / Sun	Sat / Sun	Sat / Sun
H18 L15 / H24 L14	H22 L14 / H22 L14	H22 L14 / H25 L16	H22 L14 / H22 L14
Dublin	**Madrid**	**Paris**	**Rome**
Sat / Sun	Sat / Sun	Sat / Sun	Sat / Sun
H18 L12 / H19 L11	H23 L15 / H25 L16	H32 L25 / H32 L24	H22 L15 / H24 L15

Oslo 18 64 Fair
Well'ton 15 59 Fair
Zurich 17 63 Rain

No 2.

4

You will LOVE the South of France!!!

Hooray! Mr. Bean is coming!

Excellent! When?

Best sweep the floor! He doesn't like it dirty!

What does he eat?

Best get to the shops!

What does he look like?

Like this stupid!

6

7

MAKE A LIST OF THINGS TO TAKE.

Yourself (Myself)
Jacket
Fridge
Shirt
Tie
Trousers
Socks x2
Record Player
Pants x???
Vests x???
Wardrobe
Towel
Bed
Bucket and Spade
Disgusting Powdered Mountaineer's food
Dressing gown
Sun Hat
Sun Cream
Ice Cream
Carrots
Gravy
Chicken
* Swimming trunks
Beans (tins of, not me's of)
Cooker
Sun Glasses
Sausages
Tent?
Fish fingers
TV Set
Foot Powder
Frozen Peas
Camping stove?
SUITCASE!

*If by chance
you're going to France
Don't forget
Your under-pance!
(A poem by Mr. Bean)*

*NOTE TO SELF –
BUY SOME (CHEAP!)*

*This book
is going
quite well,
I think*

Swimwear

How to decide what trunks suit you without having to try the ruddy things on!

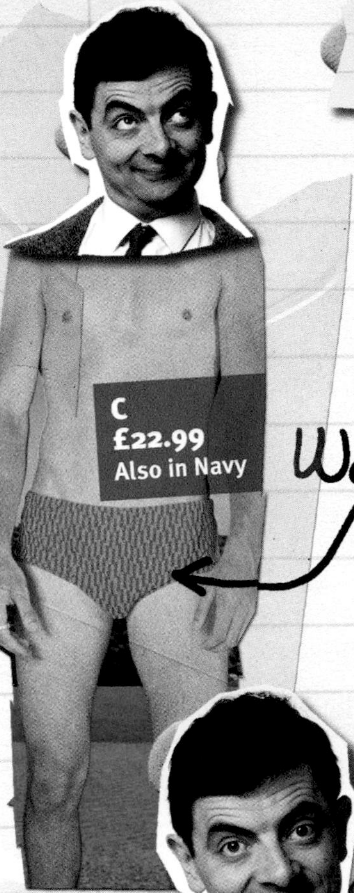

C
£22.99
Also in Navy

Women's?

F
£17.99
Also in Cerise

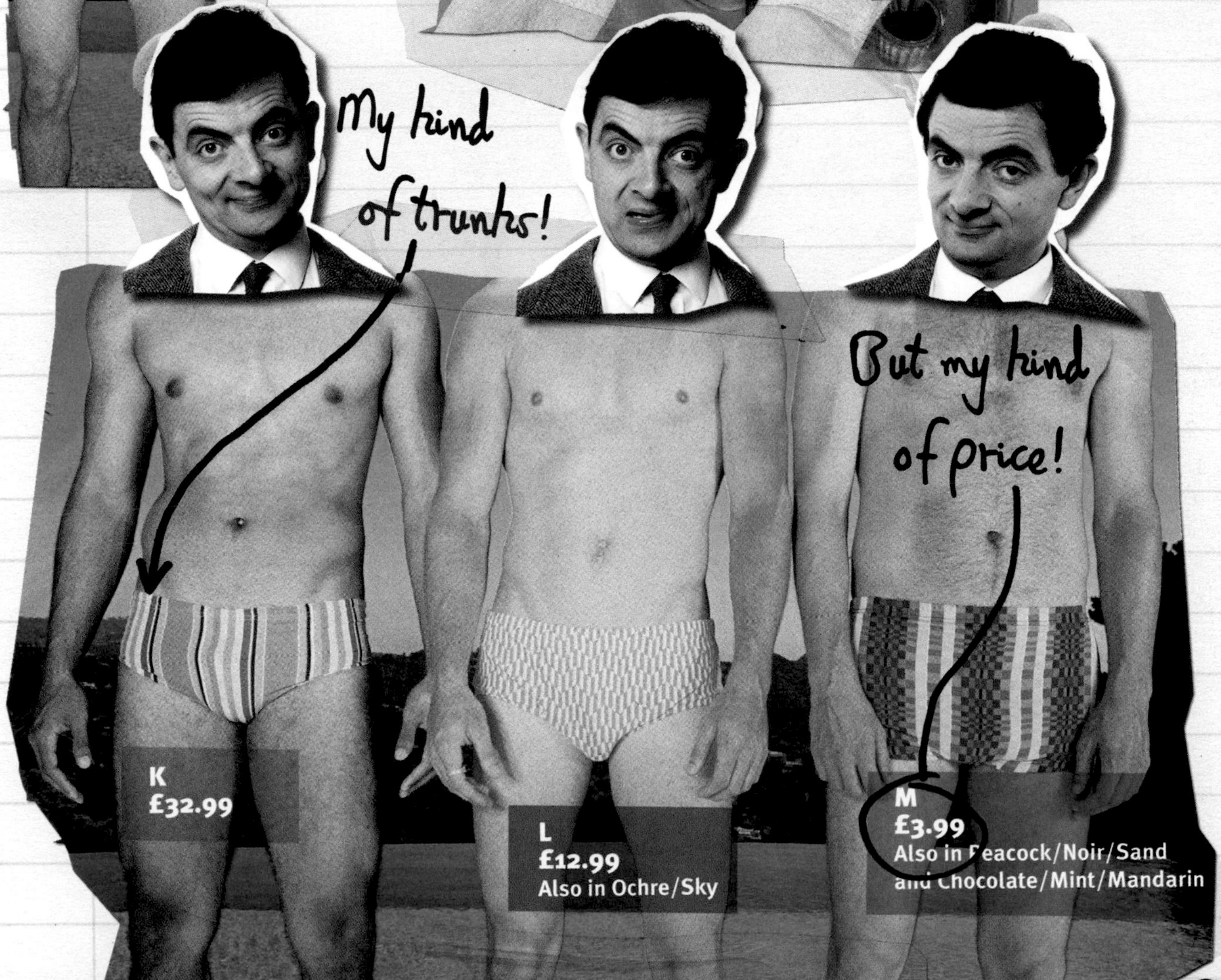

My kind of trunks!

But my kind of price!

K
£32.99

L
£12.99
Also in Ochre/Sky

M
£3.99
Also in Peacock/Noir/Sand and Chocolate/Mint/Mandarin

'Daffodils'
12 Arbour Road
Highbury
London N10
England.

15th April 2006
London Passport Office
Globe House
89 Eccleston Square
London.

Dear Sir or Madam,

COPY

I will be popping off to France shortly and would like a passport for my bear.

Therefore, re the above, could you please send me the appropriate application form for the aforementioned passport for the aforementioned bear. Gracias (as they say in France).

Yours Sincer

Mr. Bea

Mr. Bean

COPY

Mr. Bean
c/o Mrs. Wicket
'Daffodils'
12 Arbour Road
Highbury
London N10
England.

May 15th 2006

Throne Room
Buckingham Palace
London.

Dear Your Majesty,

Hope you are well, I am fine.

Just to let you know that I'll be out of the country on a short break, as twer. France, don't ya know. So if you want to call me for a chat, as twer, that's why nobody'll be answering the phone, as twer.

Your Loyal Servant,

M. B

STEP 3:

Understanding the currency of
France!
(That means 'money' in English.)

Ours

Theirs

Euros Euros all around
Where O where's my lovely Pound?
(A poem by Mr. Bean)

Home Office

Nasty Office more like it!

April 21st, 2006

Mr. Bean
c/o Mrs. Wicket
'Daffodils'
12 Arbour Road
Highbury
London N10

RE: Your bear.

Dear Mr. Bean,

Your letter of the 15th has been passed on to me by the Duty Manager of the Passport Service Office, Putney. I was extremely alarmed by your letter and by the casualness with which you seek to illegally transport your bear abroad.

The creature's potential suffering aside, the export of any animal is strictly forbidden without the proper permits and the strictest of quarantine arrangements.

Be warned, Sir, that if you are caught transporting your bear to France you will face criminal proceedings that will definitely lead to a heavy fine or a prison sentence.

I have entered your name into our nationwide database and have alerted all British ports, airports and other points of departure.

Yours faithfully,

Rupert Fleecing

Rupert Fleecing.
(Chief Policy Enforcer.)

Kennels?
Cattery?
Shoebox?

Break bad news to Teddy (gently)

ITINERARARARYRARY:

Night before:

10pm	Pack suitcase.(see list of things to take.)
10.05	Put train tickets on kitchen table.
10.15	Go to bed.
10.16	Set alarm clock.
10.17	Sleep.

DAY ← 100 feet

The Big Day:

7.00	Wake up.
7.05	Wake up.
7.10	RUDDY WAKE UP AGAIN!
7.11	Run bath.
7.12	Dress.
7.15	Brush teeth.
7.16	Get undressed again (and have bath).
7.45	1st cup of tea.
7.47	1st piece of toast. (Jam.)
7.49	2nd cup of tea.
7.51	2nd piece of toast. (Marmalade.)
7.55	Turn off water.
8.00	Turn off gas.
8.01	Drive to station.
8.45	Drive back from station.
8.46	Collect train tickets from kitchen table.
8.47	Leave for station.
8.48	Go back for bag.
8.49	Leave for station.
1.00pm	Arrive in Paris.
2.05pm	Get train to South of France. (Beach!!!)
2.06pm	Try to remember if you turned off gas.

One of the unfortunate facts in going
abroad is that some travelling is involved.
Oh that it could be this easy!

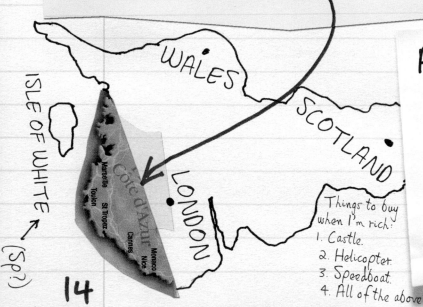

All very interesting
stuff for the reader.
YES!
I shall publish!!

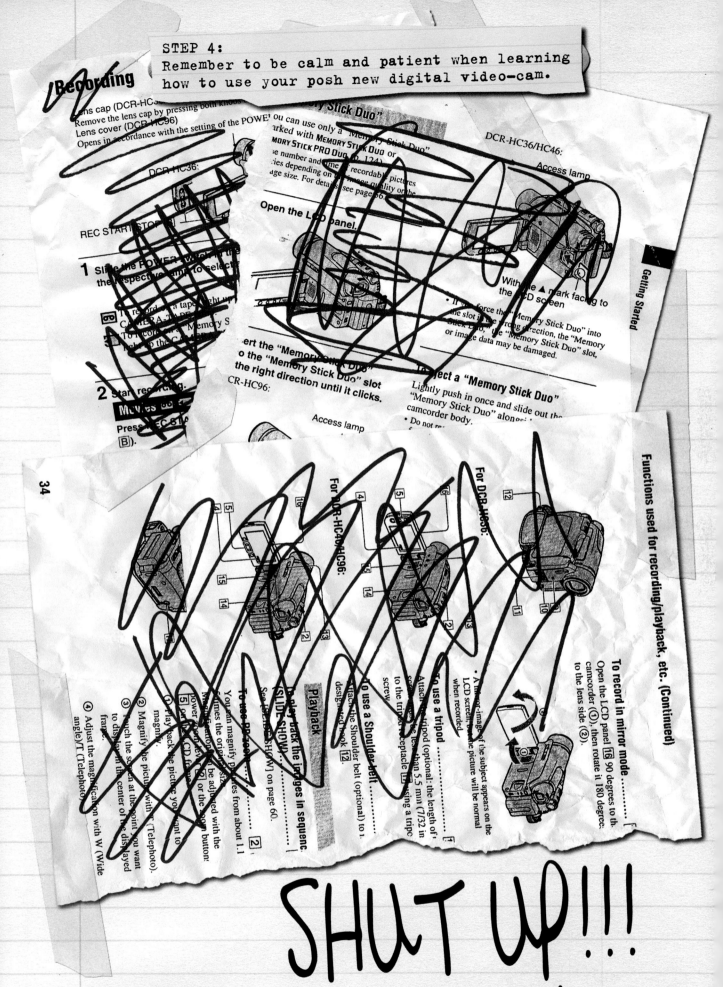

STEP 4:
Remember to be calm and patient when learning how to use your posh new digital video-cam.

SHUT UP!!!
ON & OFF will do!!

Mmm... seems very nice

COPY

Mr. Bean
c/o Mrs. Wicket
'Daffodils'
12 Arbour Road
Highbury
London N10
England.

April 27th 2006

The President
of France's house,
France.

Dear President Chirac,

I hope you are well, I am fine.

Just dropping you a line to say that I'll be down
in your neck of the woods (France) in a few days'
time. Can't wait actually. All that sun, sea and
palm trees. Smashing!

As well as enjoying a lovely sunny holiday, I
will never the less be on the lookout for any
improvements that can be made to your country.

Yours Sincerely,

Mr. Bean

Mr. Bean (of England).

P.S. Regards to the Missus.

COPY

Mr. Bean
c/o Mrs. Wicket
'Daffodils'
12 Arbour Road
Highbury
London N10
England.

May 30th 2006

Dear Lord Bloomsbury,

You don't know me (yet) but I'm the bloke that's going to make us millions!

How? Well, I shall be holidaying in France shortly and plan to write a book about it.

You see, it struck me that so many people like travelling and reading books. So why not have a book about travelling? You see my logic, my Lord?

I think your Lordship has been missing a hole in the market. So come on old boy, let's clean up!

Yours in humbleness,

Mr. Bean

Mr. Bean (Travel Writer.)

Bean on the phone President Chirac.

Excellent! Send the helicopter.

Your wife's gone shopping in it.

Hooraay!!!
Camera up and running!

My new camera does still pictures as well as video!

It can even take pictures of food!

You can use it without even looking at the instructions.

Hang on! My teapot wasn't out of focus when I bought it.

Neither was my toaster!!

All right I'll read the ruddy instructions!!!

20

Waterloo Station was designed by the same bloke who did Buckingham Palace.

The bloke who did Buckingham Palace.

The Battle of Waterloo.

Charge!!!!

Water in the loo.

21

MR. BEAN'S GUIDE TO WHAT'S GOOD, BAD, OR INDIFFERENT

People abroad will really value your opinion of their country! Why not try these handy symbols for yourself?

EXCELLENT

HARD TO RESIST

AS GOOD AS FISH AND CHIPS

AVERAGE

NICE

A JOKE

BAD

SHOULD BE THROWN OFF A CLIFF

PILE OF POO

23

toilettes

On arriving in Paris, any travel writer worth his salt
will notice that there's no beach!!!

Can't wait!

French

Not to worry. You just get a
taxi (same word in English)
across the city to Gare de Lyon
station where a train will take
you to one!!!

Unless the stupid taxi driver
doesn't understand a word you
say and dumps you somewhere
like this.

???

ound • Beach voll

playground • Table teng

6/5 8

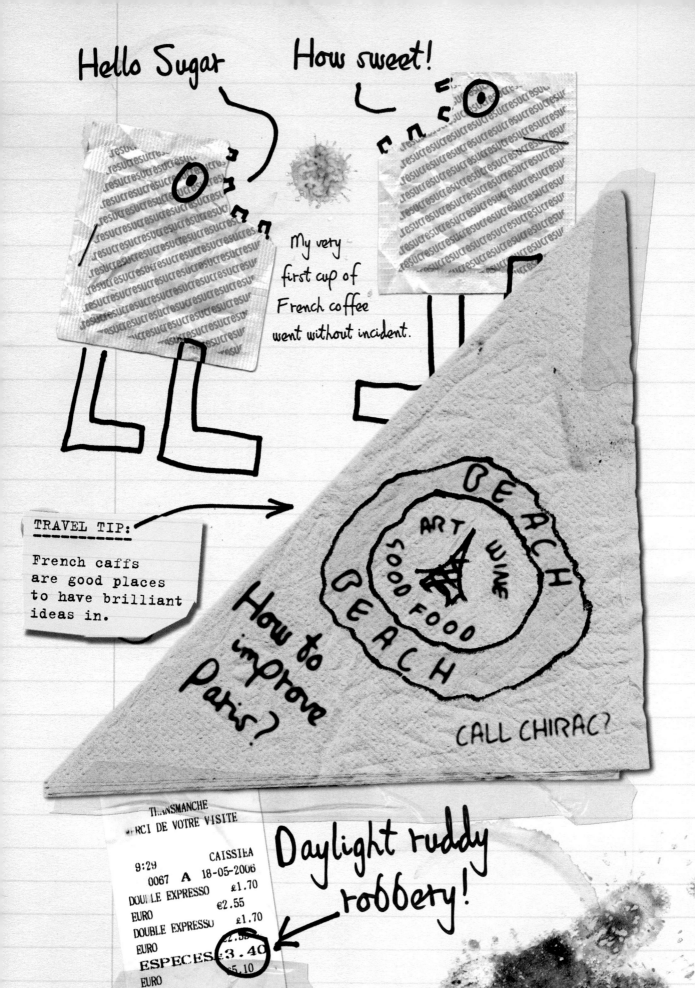

Hello Sugar

How sweet!

My very first cup of French coffee went without incident.

TRAVEL TIP:

French caffs are good places to have brilliant ideas in.

How to improve Paris?

BEACH
BEACH
ART WINE
GOOD FOOD

CALL CHIRAC?

TRANSMANCHE
MERCI DE VOTRE VISITE

9:29   CAISSIEA
  0067 A 18-05-2006
DOUBLE EXPRESSO   £1.70
EURO   €2.55
DOUBLE EXPRESSO   £1.70
EURO   €2.55
ESPECES€3.40
EURO   €5.10

Daylight ruddy robbery!

In order to avoid misunderstandings it's not a bad idea for the 'would-be' traveller to brush up his French, as Admiral Lord Nelson once said.

The only three words you need (to get by) in France, or indeed anywhere abroad are:

"OUI"   "NON"   "GRACIAS"
  ↓   ↓   ↓
"Yes"   "No"   "Thank you"

PRONUNCIATION TIP
The best way to sound like a real French person is to practise speaking with a clothes peg on your nose.
(Remove peg before you get to Passport Control.)

YOU ARE NOW READY TO TEST WHAT YOU HAVE LEARNT,
BY TICKING THE APPROPRIATE BOXES:

	OUI	NON	GRACIAS
Is my name Mr. Bean?	☐	☐	☐
Are you enjoying this test?	☐	☐	☐
What do you say to Mr. Bean for teaching you the language?	☐	☐	☐

FOR ANOTHER GOOD TIP, SEE BELOW:

French people like you to shout!

(WHISPER) GRACIAS.

GRACIAS!

Paris
Tour Eiffel

Dear Teddy,
you wouldn't like
it here,
SO SHUT UP!
from Guess who?

Teddy c/o Mrs Wichet,
'Daffodils',
12 Arbour Road,
Highbury,
London N10
ENGLAND

Dear Your Majesty,

Having a nice time in France.

You should bring Phil

here for a slap up nosh!

Mr. Bean xxx

(your humble servant.)

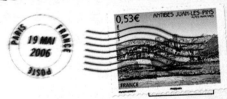

The Queen,
Buckingham Palace,
London,
ENGLAND

A LA CARTE MENU

MOULES?
MULES?
MARINERE?
MARINERS

Seafaring
Donkeys?

LES HORS D'OEUVRES
Moules Mariniere
Souffle au fromage
Mousse de Saumon et Capres
Cassolette d'escargots Les
Gratinee a l'Oignon

POISON???

LES POISSONS
Blanquette de Lotte a la Vapeur, Raviole au Petit Poits
et Emulsion au Gingembre
Bar Roti au Jeune Poireaux, Reduction de Beaujolias
et Epedutres a la Crème

Inspector?

St. Bernard – Dog?

LES ENTREES
Entrecote Grille Sauce Bearnaisse et Pommes Allumettes
Coq au Vin de Bourgogne
Jarret de Porc Confit aux Lentilles Vertes du Puy

LES POMMES DE TERRE
Gratin Dauphinois
Pommes Sautees

Grated
DOLPHINS?

Aussie
Talk?

LES LEGUMES
Petit Pois
Haricots Verte
Epinard a la Crème

Leg Room?

Varicose hurt? (veins?)

3

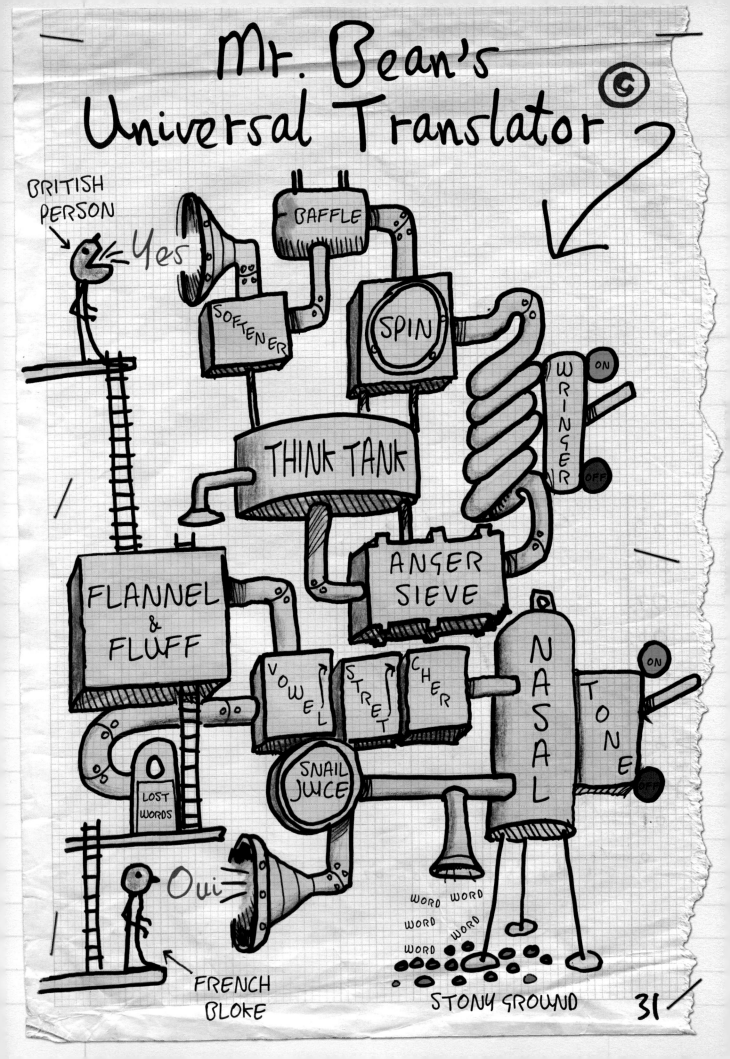

For the man who travels light! ↓

(cup of...tee hee...)

Mr. Bean
c/o Mrs. Wicket
'Daffodils'
12 Arbour Road
Highbury
London N10
England.

COPY

June 6th, 2006

United Nations H.Q.
Manhattan
New York
U.S.A.

Dear Kofi Annan,

How are things at the good old U.N.? The state of the world eh? Dear oh dear oh dear.

Anyway, like me, I bet you stay awake at night wishing that everyone could speak everybody else's language and this is where my brainwave comes in: 'The Mr. Bean's Universal Translator' (blueprint enclosed).

If everyone had one of these we'd be laughing! This is all 'TOP SECRET' at the moment so keep your trap shut okay?

Yours,

Mr. Bean

Mr. Bean (A.A. R.A.C. T.S.B.)

P.S. Obviously, this idea is worth billions but I'm more interested in doing my bit for world peace. A pint of beer would suffice.

Spare !

(MOANING LISA IN FRENCH)

TRANSLATION:

In (June) of (1445) Leonardo Da Vinci planned to put an (egg) in the painting. But a (female) person told him to use (pâté) instead. Leonardo then changed the pâté to a (jammy) (eclair), but thought it looked (amateurish).

(That's why there isn't any food in the painting.)

La Joconde de Léonard da Vinci est l'(œuvre) la plus documentée du monde. Ce portrait d'une jeune femme souriante mais inconnue a été reproduite (maint)e (fois) par les publicitaires. D'après Vasari, ce portrait serait celui d'une jeune Florentine qui épousa Francesco del Giocondo en (1445). L'exécution du tableau se situe dans la deuxième période Florentine peintre. Il est considéré comme le portrait le plus représentant de la période de la Renaissance ainsi qui l'œuvre la plus copiée et la plus admirée Le tableau acquis une certaine notoriété en 1911 quand il fut dérobé du Louvre, mais retrouvé deux ans plus tard dans un hôtel de Florence. La force du tableau est dans la sourire énigmatique de la jeune (femme), un mystère que ne sera sans doute (jamais) (éclairci) mais fascinera les (amateurs) d'art d'aujourd'hui et de demain.

'THE MOANING LISA'

I'm so fed up. I can't tell you how fed up I am. Really, really fed up to the back teeth.

33

YOU ARE HERE.

THE LOUVRE.

See if you can find your way to The Louvre.

It took me ALL RUDDY AFTERNOOOOOOOON!!!!!!!!

AFFIX
CHEAP
STAMP
HERE

IMPROVED BY MR. BEAN (OF LONDON)

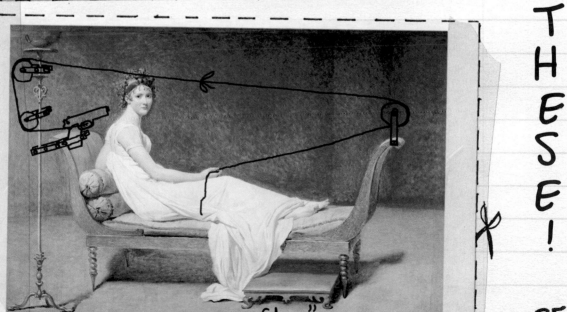

Officer of the Hussars.
IMPROVED BY MR. BEAN (OF LONDON)

On The Beach.
IMPROVED BY MR. BEAN (OF LONDON)

Madame Recaimet.
IMPROVED BY MR. BEAN (OF LONDON)

MR. BEAN'S HOLIDAY TIPS - NUMBER ONE

If like me you are too mean and tight-fisted to buy postcards, why not make your own?

Mr. Bean

Mr. Bean

France is a land of great art, great food and great wine, so why not have fun by putting them all together?

THE TASTEFUL FRENCH COUNTRYSIDE

← THIS WAY UP!

FARMER SPROUT IN HIS TRACTOR.

Now raid mummy's cupboards and make your own mess art.

In Paris, art is such the rage that people are even doing people's portraits in the streets!
A good way of earning a little extra spending money is to also try your hand at sketching tourists' portraits.

Maurice somebody.

by Mr. Bean ©

MR. BEAN'S TIP ON DOING PEOPLE'S SKETCH PORTRAITS

If people are ugly try to make them better looking, as then they will be more likely to buy your portrait.

Sunny Bliss

I Can't Wait!

Mr. Bean's gone to the South of France.
Yes. It'll be so boring without him.
The economy will suffer.
Sob, sob...
Oh shut up!
Where is the South of France?
South, stupid.
Paris has lost its greatest jewel.
Doubt it.

These excellent high speed TGV trains travel at an astonishing 200mph (320kph in the metric system!)

200 mph.

200 mph.

He never spills a drop!

MR. BEAN'S HOLIDAY TIPS - NUMBER THREE

To not feel sick imagine wearing a jet pack and travelling at 200mph backwards at the same time! (See Fig.1).

Fig.1

200mph

= Not feeling sick

200mph

JET PAK

3

MR. BEAN'S HOLIDAY TIPS - NUMBER FOUR

Make other people take photographs of you, or your holiday album will be full of total ruddy strangers.

Me on Gare de Lyon train station.

MR. BEAN'S HOLIDAY TIPS - NUMBER FIVE

To stop people running off and stealing your camera, (see Fig.2).

Ditto.

Thankyou CLICK!

Fig. 2

Ditto, ditto.

Me on the very fast
TGV train to the South
of France.
(PHOTO TAKEN BY STEPAN)

It's a burney
rabbeet, oui?

Nope, Stegosaurus.

Ditto.
Plus irritating ticket inspector.
(PHOTO TAKEN BY STEPAN)

This is Stepan!
(PHOTO TAKEN BY ME.)

(Stepan was an excellent chap to meet on my travels even
though he couldn't speak a ruddy word of English.)

Jacques Chirac
President of France
Head of the Government
Paris

May 30th, 2006

Mr. Bean,

Your letter has been received. Thank you for sending it.

You will appreciate that President Chirac is far too busy running the country to reply to you in person.

Yours faithfully

Claude De Rebuffet

Claude De Rebuffet.
3rd Secretary to the 4th Assistant Secretary
to President Chirac's 5th Under Secretary.

KILLER BEES

CLOSE
OPEN

CHATEAU CHIRAC.

THE UNITED NATIONS
From The Office of Kofi Annan
Secretary General

Two jobs?

Too busy to write a proper letter!

Dear Mr. Bean

Thank you for your letter.

Yours Faithfully

Kofi Annan

Kofi Annan
Secretary General of The U

COPY

United Nations H.Q.
Manhattan
New York
U.S.A.

Mr. Be
c/o Mr
Daffoc
12 Arbo
Highbur
London N10
England.

19th June, 2006

Dear Kofi,

If it's the size of my 'Universal Translator',
that's giving you the collywobbles, then please
see the new plans (enclosed).

Yours again
(for Heaven's sake),

M R A C

. R.A.C.

47

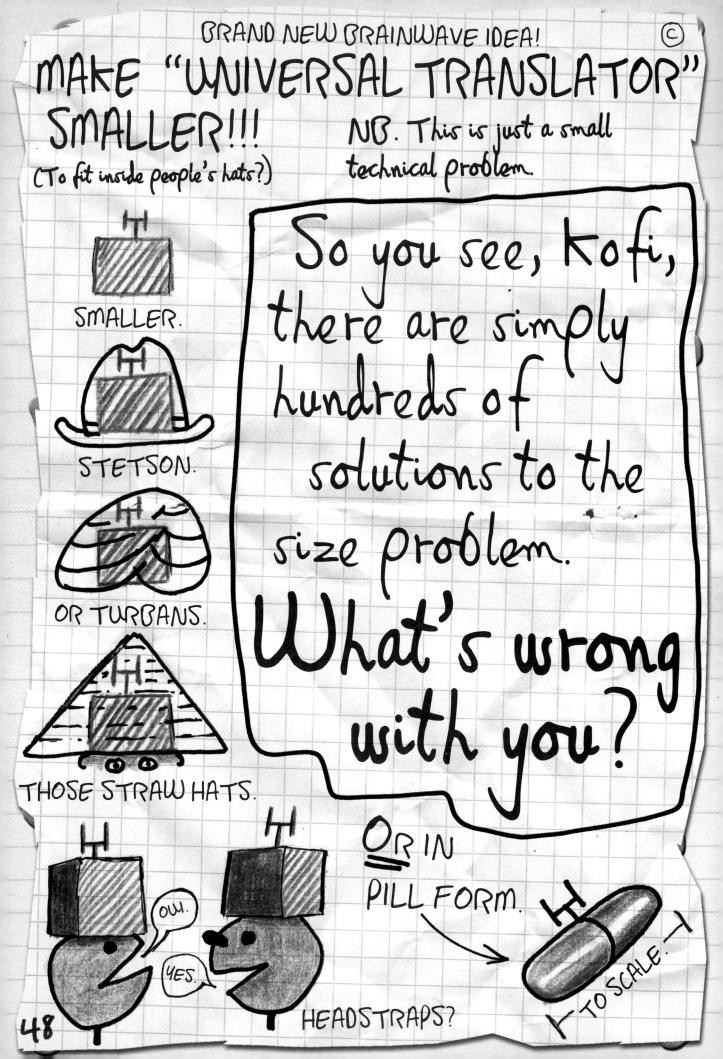

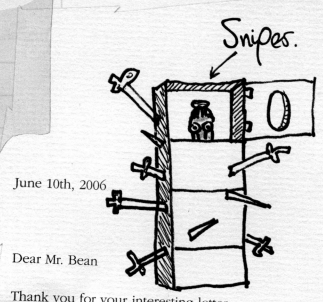

Snipes.

BLOOMSBURY

June 10th, 2006

Dear Mr. Bean

Thank you for your interesting letter.

Bloomsbury Publishing is well aware of the travel book market.

We publish a wide selection of such books and have a plethora of experienced travel writers and do not need any more.

Yours faithfully

Wendy Snipes
Assistant Secretary to
Jonathan Groan
(Head of Nuisance Letters Dep...

Mr. Bean
c/o Mrs. Wicket
'Daffodils'
12 Arbour Road
Highbury
London N10
England.

12th June, 2006

...blishing
...o Square
London W1D 3QY

Dear Ms. Snipes,

It's all very nice hearing it from the 'monkey' (you) but I'd rather hear it from the 'organ grinder' (Lord Bloomsbury) if you don't mind, young lady.

Mr. Bean

Mr. Bean (Travel Writer. A.A. R.A.C. T.S.B.)

49

BIRD POO BATTLESHIPS

An original and exciting version of the boring old Battleships game, for 2 players.

© Mr. Pam

INSTRUCTIONS

1. Sit opposite from your opponent.

2. Hold up page 51-52 between you, so there's no peeking. (See Fig. 1)

3. Each player takes turn to name a square (A1, B2, C3, D2, etc.)

4. If there's a cake on that square BIRD POO has landed on it!!!!!!

5. Scribble out that square!!!!!

6. OR: Tear out a small piece of white paper and place that on the square. (small piece of white paper = bird poo)

7. The first player to get bird poo on all their cakes, LOSES!!!!!!!

Fig. 1

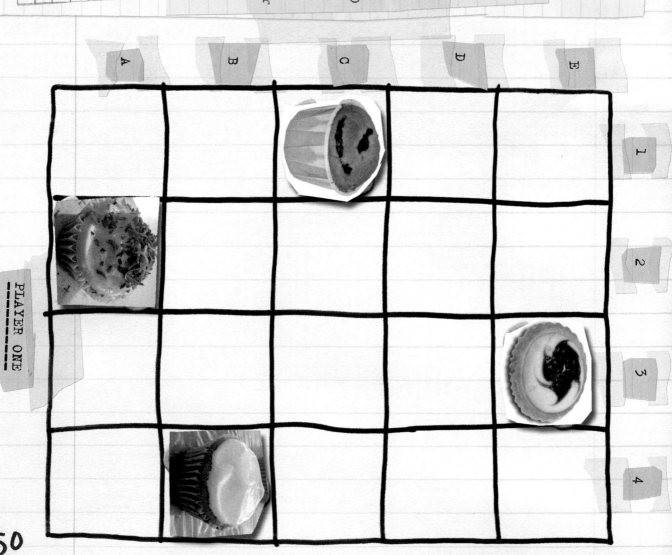

PLAYER ONE

A B C D E

1 2 3 4

50

TRADITIONAL FRENCH TRAVEL GAMES!

fun!

fun for all the family!!!

FINGER COUNTING (1 Player):

Count all the fingers on your hands. If you do it very slowly, this enjoyable pastime will last for the whole journey.

fun!

FINGER COUNTING (2 Players):

Especially good fun on long journeys. When you have counted all of your fingers, you can count your friend's fingers.

fun! *fun!*

ALTERNATIVE 'I-SPY':

This game is just like the ordinary 'I-Spy' but you cheat. For example, you say: "I spy with my little eye something beginning with P!" But the thing is, you haven't even thought of anything beginning with P! Whatever objects your playmates offer up, you just keep saying no! You can keep this going for hours and ruddy hours and when your parents finally give up and ask you what object you were thinking of, you just say you've forgotten. THAT'LL DRIVE THEM REALLY WILD!!!

fun! *fun!*

THE SONG GAME (1 Player):

Sing '10 Green Bottles', but start at a million. When no one joins in, keep going.

THE SONG GAME (2 Players):

Sing '10 Green Bottles', but start at one hundred, and your friend starts at seventy-five. This stops parents getting sleepy.

Even more fun!

THE PRETTY CROSSWORD GAME (1 Player):

There is always a posh-looking businessman asleep on your train.
1. Nick his newspaper and find the crossword page.
2. Make it look pretty by colouring in all the white squares.
3. Sneak the newspaper back onto the man's lap while he's still sleeping. Just wait to see his face when he wakes up and sees the pretty crossword.

e.g.

(Or, for more fun, make sure you colour over all the clue numbers while you're at it. The posh businessman will be pretty cross!)

wasn't that FUN!!!

THE PHONE GAME

(1 Player, I've seen kids on trains having loads of fun with this one):

TRA-LA-LA-LA-LA

Take out your mobile phone. Find the menu with the ringtone thingies. Turn up the volume really loud and go through all the ringtones in the phone. Especially fun when everyone else is trying to sleep.

PLAYER TWO

53

The beautiful French countryside.

What was your score? Be honest!

This is a game of skill, not a game of cheating!

Don't cheat!

Are you keeping score?

Try to miss the American tourists on your way to the Eiffel Tower.

If you prop this side of the book up against the train seat in front you can pretend to be tapping away on a lap-top computer like all the other posers in the train carriage. Be sure to tap loudly and to tut a lot under your breath.

MR. BEAN'S PICTURE CONSEQUENCES

There is the long way of describing how to play this game:
a. me writing all the difficult instructions
or the quick way:
b. you asking someone who already knows how to play it.
I recommend option b.
Below are a couple of examples that me and Stepan (a fellow
traveller) knocked up whilst on the train.

Also, try cutting along the dotted lines on the opposite page (59)
and fold back the flaps. The fun you will have could last up to a
whole minute!

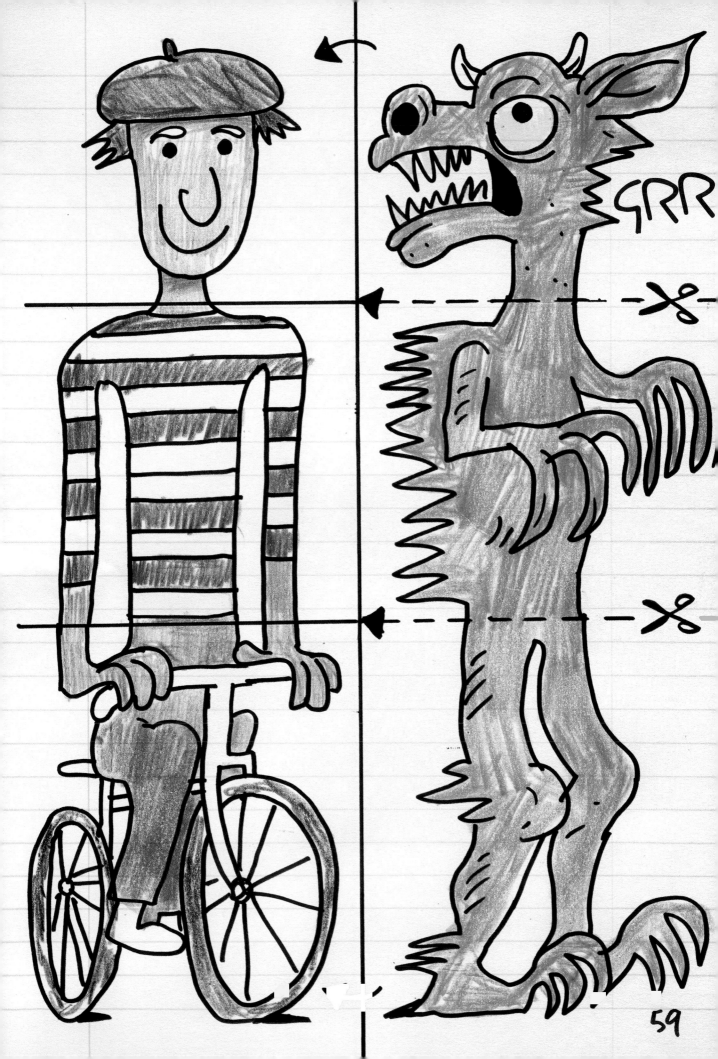

GRR

59

TEDDY

The French can be as picky about foreigners as they are about their grub and grog, but if you stick this mask on your face you should have no problem with them. (And if you're ugly you'd best stick it on anyway.)

61

MAKE YOUR VERY OWN MOANING LIZA © Mr. Bean

Now everyone can own a priceless masterpiece!
And all you need is a pair of scissors and some glue!
When you have assembled it, why not hang it in your own Louvre?

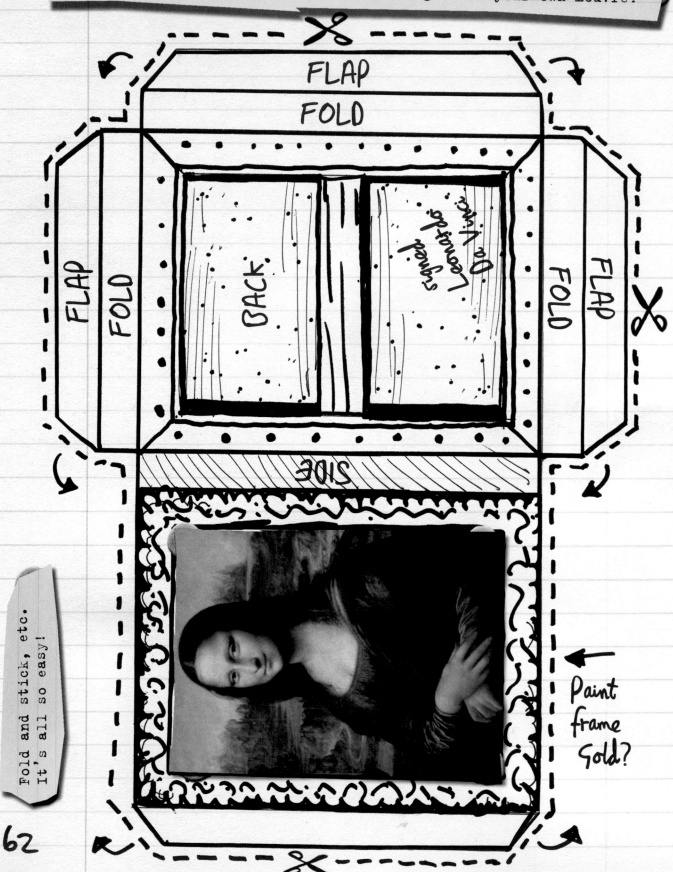

FLAP
FOLD

FLAP
FOLD

BACK

Leonardo Da Vinci

FLAP
FOLD

SIDE

Fold and stick, etc.
It's all so easy!

Paint frame Gold?

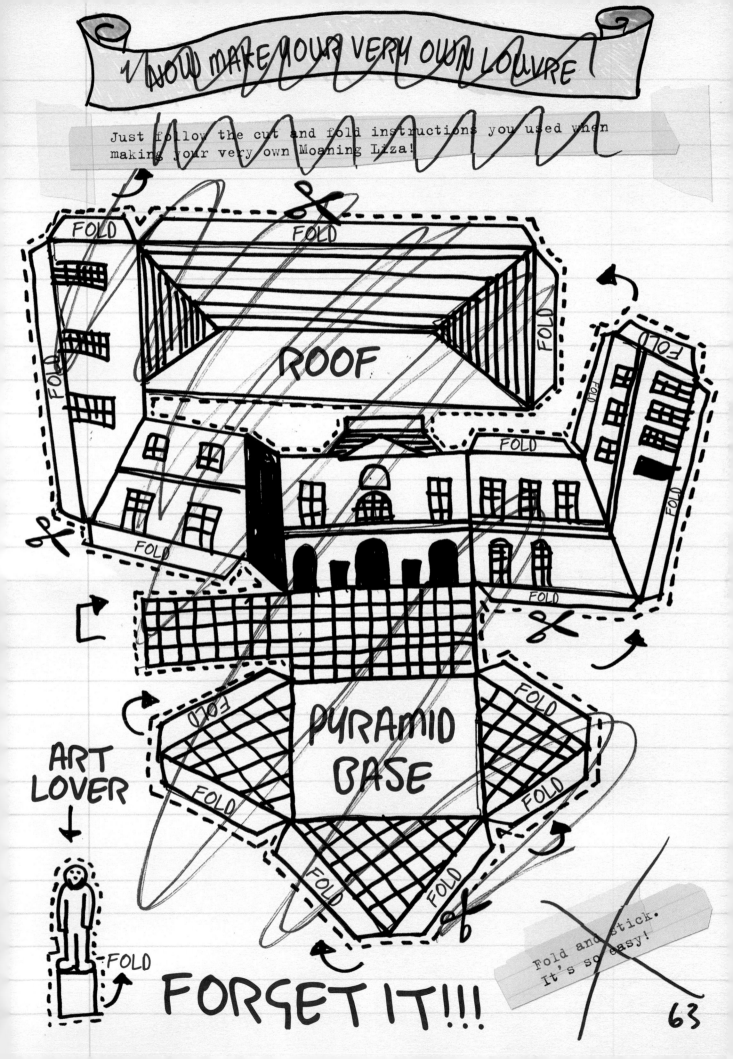

NOW MAKE YOUR VERY OWN LOUVRE

D-I-Y BORING PHOTO COMPETITION

Don't discard all your boring photographs. Compare them with your mates' throwaways and think up a prize to give for the most boringest entry. The prize could just be a cup of tea, or even better – a slap up plate of fish and chips, with mushy peas and two rounds of bread and butter (pickled onion optional). Yum!

If your photos aren't as boring as these...
Give me the fish and chips if you please!

65

66

THE GREAT FISH AND CHIP HUNT!

9am: Onions and garlic all around, but fish and chips cannot be found!

9.15am: "Fish and chips sir, if you please?" But all he had was smelly cheese!

10.02am: He told me to go next door, where, all they had was more cheese (in there!)

10.30am: Peaches? No, no, I want chips!

10.45am: I haven't got time to make this rhyme, because it's 10.45 and I've got to get going!

11.05am: Oh where, oh where are my lovely fish and chips?

11.20am: Thought about catching a fish.
11.21am: Gave up on the idea.

11.45am: The road to utter despair is fish and chip-less.

He'll have to make do with Coq au Vin.

Cock o' what?

Nah... Still ruddy holding.

69

You may not be as lucky as me in going to France and experiencing the "Real Thing", as it were, so here's how to make some authentic French stuff at home.

COQ → 🐔🍷 ← AU VIN

1. GET A CHICKEN DRUNK ON RED WINE.
2. WAIT TILL CHICKEN FALLS ASLEEP AND WRING ITS NECK.
3. IF YOU ARE SQUEAMISH GET SOMEONE ELSE TO WRING ITS NECK.
4. OR GET AN ALCOHOLIC CHICKEN THAT WAS DYING ANYWAY.
5. OR GET ONE FROM THE SHOPS (RECOMMENDED).
6. FRY ONIONS AND GARLIC IN BIG PAN.
7. ADD CHICKEN.
8. ADD BOTTLE OF RED WINE.
9. SIMMER FOR TWO HOURS.
10. ADD MORE WINE.
11. HAVE A SIP OF WINE YOURSELF.
12. SIMMER FOR AN HOUR.
13. GO OUT AND GET MORE WINE!
14. ADD MORE WINE.
15. SIMMER FOR TWO HOURS.
16. SERVE WITH A GLASS OF WINE.
17. It's absolutely DeeeLicious!

I just dashed this recipe off in a cafe, as twer.

70

The French have absolutely millions of different types of wine, but they can be expensive, so here is how to make your own French wine at home, with what you have in the cupboard.

Rinse out a bottle and add to it:

a.) 1 teaspoon of cocoa.
b.) 1 teaspoon of sugar.
c.) a half teaspoon of raspberry jam.
d.) 5 teaspoons of melted ice cream.
e.) Fill to the top with orange juice.
f.) Shake well for 2 mins and put in fridge for 2 hrs.
g.) Add French vinegar to taste (or not).

How the French get their cheeses quite so smelly is a closely guarded secret. This is my method:

1. Take an ordinary piece of (non smelly) cheese.
2. Take one smelly sock. (NB: for extra flavour try wearing your socks for 2 or 3 days.)
3. Insert cheese into sock (see Fig. 1).
4. Leave in a sunny spot for 2 days (bring in at night).
5. Remove the cheese from the sock before serving. Enjoy your friends' comments on how much it stinks!

(Fig. 1.)

THE UNITED NATIONS
From The Office of Kofi Annan
Secretary General

Rats!

Rats!

June 23rd , 2006

RATS!

Dear Mr. Bean

Thank you for your letter.

Yours Faithfully

Kofi Annan

Kofi Annan
Secretary General of The United Nations

This makes me so

MAD!

Dear Your Majesty,
(& Phil) Having a lovely
time except that Kofi
Annan will not look at
my idea for world peace.
Do you have any clout
with him? *Mr. Bean*
xxx

Her Majesty,
Buckingham Palace,
London,
ENGLAND

0.53€ ANTIBES JUAN-LES-PINS

PARIS FRANCE
26 MAI
2006
POSTE

Dear Your Majesty,
(& Phil) As I was
saying, I'm a bit fed
up. Do you know Lord
Bloomsbury? Could you
put a rocket up him?

Mr. Bean xxx

Her Majesty,
Buckingham Palace,
London,
ENGLAND

(CONT:)

You take the bother to
write to these bods and
all you get is rudeness.
Take President Chirac.
(Please!)   xxx

(CONT:)

Her Majesty,
Buckingham Palace,
London,
ENGLAND

By the way, could you
and Phil let me have
these postcards back
when I get back home.
I'll need them for my
travel book.
xxx

(If Lord Bloomsbury

Her Majesty,
Buckingham Palace,
London,
ENGLAND

pulls his finger out!)

73

74

At last! Civilisation!

Tut! Will have to ruddy hitch.

Dum-de-dum de-dum...

La-la-la-de-de-dum-dum...

Diddly-do-do-te-tum...

Come on, come on...

Look, look, look...

Hooray! And just like the lovely car I've got at home!

And this is Sabine, an actress on her way to the Cannes Film Festival. An excellent young woman but drives on the wrong side of the road.

My film camera by the way.

77

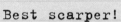

79

My camera,
by the way!

Mr. Bean
c/o Mrs. Wicket
'Daffodils'
12 Arbour Road
Highbury
London N10
England.

May 10th, 2006

Head Man/Woman,
The Cannes Film Festival,
3, rue Amélie, 750017 Paris, France (of course).

Dear Head Man/Woman,

My friend, Sabine, told me all about your excellent
film festival and it just so happens that I have a
brilliant idea for a 'Blockbuster!' (as I believe you
call them). Not to give too much away, I thought of
doing a film about a man with a big nose, but that's
already been done by you in French. So how about doing one about a man with big feet? Please see the enclosed 'Storyboard' (as I believe you call them).

I've got all the good ideas so all you have to do is
to cough up the following:
The money. The director. The cameraman. The lights.
The actors. The make-up and the scenery and
everything.

Time-wise, I've got a 'window' (as I believe you call
them) in the Autumn, between tiling the bathroom and
being in hospital for a toe operation (nothing for
you to worry about). So we can make it then, whatever
your name is.

Yours,

Mr. Bean
Mr. Bean

COPY

81

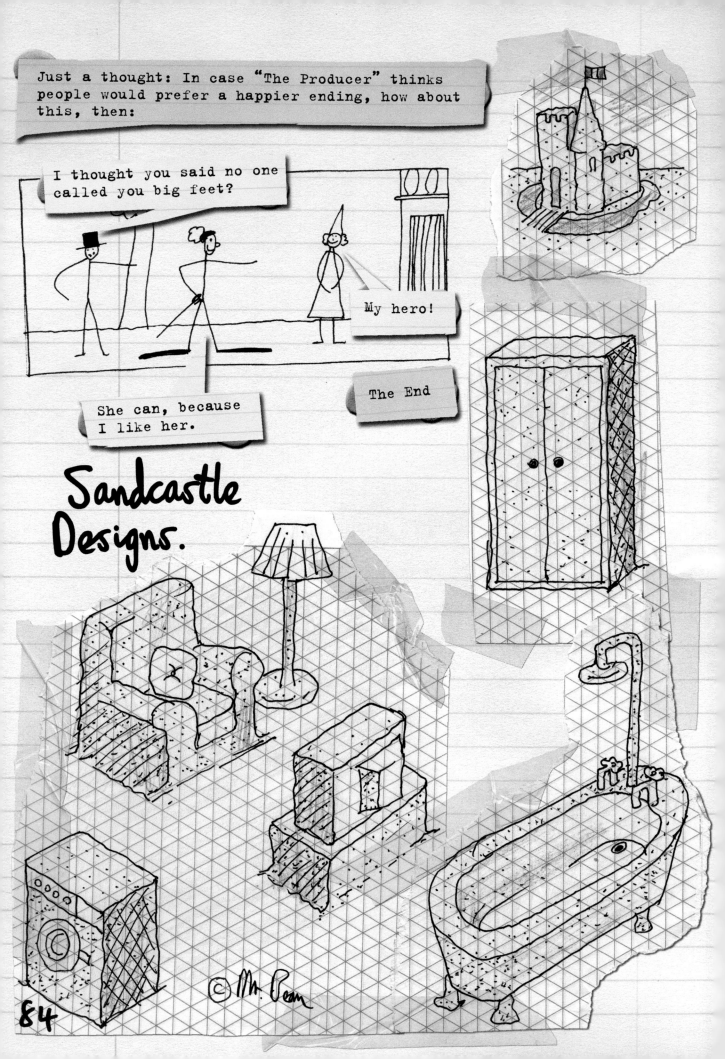

Ahhhh... My lovely friend Sabine.

And let's not forget the lovely Stepan (And lovely me, of course.)

Official Cannes sand! →

All together now... (Quite literally.)

Enough of the soppy stuff. Now back to the PADDLING!

THESE GLASSES WILL NEVER LET YOU DOWN!

If you have been stupid enough to get lost and not get to the beach, or it's ruddy raining all the time, cut these out and pop them on. Mmmmmm, lovely.

FOLD.

FOLD.

FOLD.

FOLD.

FOLD.

FOLD.

FOLD.

PICTURES ON THE INSIDE!

© Mr. Bean

88

MR. BEAN'S GUIDE TO FUN IN THE SUN

Lying in the sun can be fun, but also can get a bit boring. So why not spice up your sunbathing with these exciting sunbathing stencils?

1. Cut out the stencils.
2. Do not apply your sun tan lotion
3. Apply the stencil to your chest or back.
4. Lie in the sun (the sun will do the rest).
5. After a couple of hours remove the stencil.
6. The sun will have burnt attractive bright red patterns into your skin, that will impress your friends.

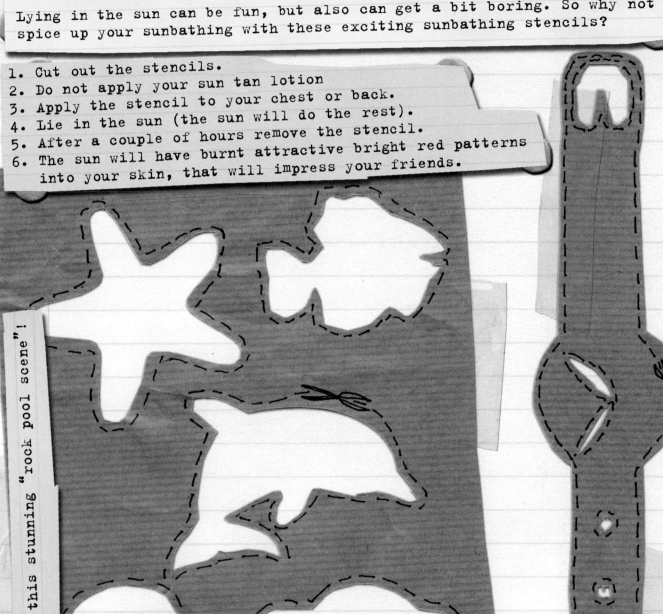

Why not try this stunning "rock pool scene"!

NB: PLEASE ASK YOUR MUMMY FOR PERMISSION!!!!

Otherwise you might burn yourself to a cinder and end up in hospital like I did!

FOOL YOUR FRIENDS WITH THIS WRISTWATCH STENCIL:
1. Attach the stencil to your wrist.
2. Leave it on all day.
3. When you remove the stencil, it will look as if you have forgotten to take off your wristwatch. Perfect for people who don't have wristwatches!

Football shirts can be expensive, so why not stick this stencil on your back and join "The Bean Team"?

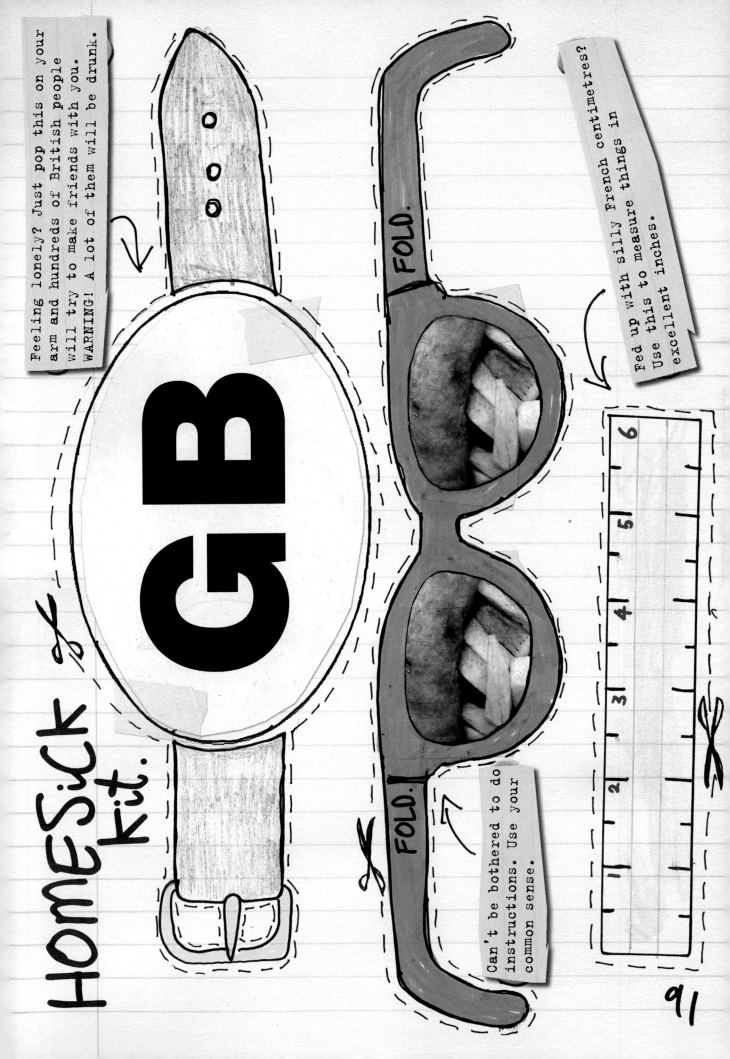

HomeSick kit.

Feeling lonely? Just pop this on your arm and hundreds of British people will try to make friends with you. WARNING! A lot of them will be drunk.

GB

FOLD.

FOLD.

Fed up with silly French centimetres? Use this to measure things in excellent inches.

Can't be bothered to do instructions. Use your common sense.

6 5 4 3 2 1

91

BLOOMSBURY

June 16th 2006

<u>Re: 'Travel Book'</u>

Dear Mr. Bean,

How many times? We're not interested!

Yours faithfully,

Snipey!   *Snipey!*

Wendy Snipes
Assistant Secretary to
Jonathan Groan
(Head of Nuisance Letters Department)

Snipey!

Snipey! *Snipey!*

Snipey!

92

E.R.

Buckingham Palace,
July 2nd 2006

Mr. Bean,
c/o Mrs. Wicket,
'Daffodils',
12 Arbour Road,
Highbury,
London N10.

Dear Mr. Bean,

Sorry not to have been in touch sooner. Phil has a nasty cold and has been a right old grump. We were both pleased to hear that you had a lovely time in France. How nice. Phil says he's very much in agreement with you regarding the Norman Invasion but forgive and forget has always been my motto.

It's been havoc here at the Palace for the last couple of weeks what with the new curtains going up, the corgis' jippy tummies, and Phil's funny bottom. What else? Oh yes, thanks for all your lovely postcards. I do indeed hear your plea and I hope you don't mind, but I've had words with the offending parties on your behalf.

And Beanie, next time you're down this way, please drop in that rhubarb recipe.

All the Best, as ever,

ER

The Queen.
P.S. Please find enclosed the fiver Phil borrowed off you for the lotto.

POO.

THE UNITED NATIONS

From The Office of Kofi Annan
Secretary General

July 20th 2006

Dear Mr. Bean

I was chatting about you on the phone to Her Majesty, Queen Elizabeth, this morning, and cannot apologise enough for your shoddy treatment by this office. I hope you'll believe me when I say that your deeply interesting letter and plans never reached me personally. The United Nations is a big place, but that is no excuse.

The idea of a "Universal Translator" device is quite brilliant!

It's certainly something that I'll personally pass on to my backroom boffins. It'll give them something to get their teeth into. As you say, a major technical problem could be the size of your proposed device, but its importance in fostering world peace is well worth the billions of American tax dollars it will take.

With your permission, sir, I'll put forward your Universal Translator idea to the Security Council the next time it meets.

When are you next in New York? You must pop in for tea and English muffins.

My mobile number is 07700 900754. Feel free to call me anytime, day or night.

Let's get this Universal Translator off the ground as soon as possible.
The peace of the world depends upon it, sir.

Yours faithfully,

Kofi Annan

Kofi.

Too late! Selling it to China!

94

BLOOMSBURY

Lovely Simpleton!

July 16th 2006

Dear Mr. Bean,

I cannot apologise enough for the rude replies you received in response to your communications with Wendy Snipes, Assistant Secretary to Jonathan Groan, Head of Nuisance Letters Department, both of whom are no longer with us.

After my delightful phone conversation with Her Majesty the Queen, I managed to track down your proposal for a travel book. What a wonderfully brilliant and inspired idea!

I talked to the board immediately and we are all in agreement that Bloomsbury is, as you have so astutely pointed out, indeed missing a hole in the market.

You'll be delighted to know that we would like to fill that hole with you.
Just send us everything you've got from the French trip. We'll publish it as soon as we can cancel some other author's project.

No need for us to meet. Cheque's in the post. (Do say if it's not enough.)

Bloomsbury Publishing welcomes you on board, Mr. Bean!

Yours faithfully,

Susan Simpleton

Susan Simpleton
(Director, Bloomsbury Publishing.)

PS: Please pass on my kind regards to Her Majesty and thank her for the rhubarb recipe.
One of yours I understand.